Mini-Moments
for
Fathers

Man to Man
Special Blessings
Pastor
Rory

Mini-Moments
for
Fathers

by Robert Strand

New Leaf Press

First printing: February 1996
Fifth printing: April 2000

ISBN: 0-89221-317-5
Library of Congress Catalog No. 95-73127

Unless noted otherwise, Bible Scripture is from the King James Version.

Printed in the United States of America.

Please visit our website for other great titles:
www.newleafpress.net

For information regarding publicity for author interviews contact Dianna Fletcher at (870) 438-5288.

Presented to:

_____

Presented by:

_____

Date:

_____

Dad's Image

It seems to go something like this when it comes to Dad:

At age 4: "My Daddy can do anything!" At age 7: "My Dad sure knows a lot, a whole lot!" At age 8: "My Dad doesn't know quite everything." At age 12: "Oh, well, naturally, my Dad doesn't know that, either." At age 14: "Oh Dad? He's just out of date, he's old-fashioned." At age 21: "Oh, that man, he's sure not with it." At age 25: "Dad, well, he does know a little bit about it." At age 35: "Before we decide what to do, we'll talk to Dad and get his ideas first." At age 50: "I wonder, what would Dad have thought about that?" At age 60: "My Dad knew something about literally everything!" At age 65: "I really wish I could talk it over with Dad just once more!"

And I'm for appreciating what a treasure we have in our fathers!

Many a boy or girl at 16 can't possibly believe that someday they will be as dumb as Dad.

Fathers, do not exasperate your children; instead, bring them up in the training and instruction of the Lord (Eph. 6:4).

Who Is the Real Father?

Some years ago, a delightful play called "Fanny" was presented on Broadway. It was the story of a young girl in love with a young man. When she told him that she was pregnant, his immediate response was to enlist in the navy and ship out to sea.

But there was another man who also knew about the situation and desired to help Fanny. He married the pregnant girl, took care of her, and when the child was born, it was given his name.

Soon after, the young sailor came back into port and discovered what had happened. He was furious and wanted his baby back. In talking over the situation with his uncle, he was asking for help so he could state his case properly. "Tell me, Uncle? Who is the real father? The one who gave the baby life or the one who buys its bibs?"

The uncle's simple reply was, "The father is the one who loves."

Love does not need proof . . . it
needs practice.

*For the Lord your God is God of gods
and Lord of lords, the great God,
mighty and awesome, who shows no
partiality and accepts no bribes. He
defends the cause of the fatherless and
the widow* (Deut. 10:17–18).

*A father who
teaches his children
responsibility provides them
with a fortune.*

"P.Q."

A father prayed for 20 years that he might be able to speak audibly with God. Finally his request was granted. He said, "God, I have three questions. First, is a thousand years with you like a second?"

God replied, "Yes, it is."

Next the man asked, "Is a million dollars to you less than a penny?"

And God replied, "Yes, it is."

Then the man asked, "God, may I have a penny?"

And God replied, "Yes, in just a second."

Waiting can be tough. How high is your "P.Q." (patience quotient)? Can you wait at a long traffic light without fuming or fussing? Waiting can build patience, strengthen faith, remind us that God is in charge, and make better fathers of us, IF we don't abort the process!

The quality of a man's life is in direct proportion to the commitment to patience, regardless of his chosen field of endeavor.

We also rejoice in our sufferings, because we know that suffering produces perseverance; perseverance, character; and character, hope. And hope does not disappoint us, because God has poured out His love into our hearts (Rom. 5:3–5).

Overloaded

This supposedly happened in Minneapolis, in the days when a father-to-be didn't get to go into the delivery room while his wife was in labor. There were a number of fathers present and one in particular was pacing back and forth when the nurse came out of the delivery room and said, "Congratulations, Dad! Your wife just had twins!"

The man, surprised, replied, "Isn't that ironic, I play baseball for the Minnesota Twins!"

A few moments later, another nurse came to another man in the waiting room. "Congratulations, sir! Your wife just gave birth to healthy triplets!"

After he gathered his composure, he said, "Imagine . . . triplets and I work for 3M!"

About that time another man darted out of his seat and

headed for the exit. The nurse shouted after him, "Is something wrong?"

Over his shoulder he replied, "I work for 7-11 and I'm getting out of here!"

A devoted husband and father is a man who stands by his wife in troubles she wouldn't have had if she hadn't married him.

He will turn the hearts of the fathers to their children, and the hearts of the children to their fathers (Mal. 4:6).

Gimpers

You'll not find one listed in the National Wildlife Federation's manual of "Rare Species." They are rare . . . like the bald eagle, "GIMPERS" are seldom seen. Occasional sightings have reportedly occurred on college campuses, business offices, athletic teams, families, or churches. If you look closely, you might recognize one among your own friends.

Okay, what is a "gimper"? Here are a few clues. Gimpers form the backbone of whatever they are a part of. One of the reasons they're so hard to spot is that they never run in herds, they're loners! Bruce Jenner is a gimper . . . Vince Lombardi qualified as a gimper . . . Jim Elliot and Nate Saint were gimper missionaries.

In some dictionaries you can find the word, "gimp" which means: "spirit, vim, vigor, ambition." Therefore, a "gimper" is a person who is committed to the core! These roots of dedication result in the fruit of determination, excellence, and achievement!

Desire is the key to motivation, but it's the determination and commitment to an unrelenting pursuit of your goal . . . a commitment to excellence . . . that will enable you to attain the success you seek. (Mario Andretti)

I can do everything through Him who gives me strength (Phil. 4:13).

*A good father will leave
his imprint on his daughter
for the rest of her life.*

James C. Dobson (1936–)

Alexander the Great

Alexander became the "Great" because his influence outlasted his battle victories. He was raised with a sense of destiny. At 20 he inherited the throne of Macedonia from his father. He then set out with 35,000 troops to conquer whatever he could. In the next 11 years he marched more than 11,000 miles, never lost a battle, and sent Greek culture throughout the world. He was adored by his troops. But by 324 B.C., Alexander's own power became too intoxicating. He withdrew from the soldier's life, declared himself the son of Zeus, and began drinking heavily.

He was in Babylon with his army in 323 BC, preparing for his next campaign, and got into a drinking contest at a banquet. He is believed to have gulped down at least six quarts of wine. The next day, he was sick, caught cold, but from his bed continued to issue orders. Within ten days of his drinkingfest, the conqueror was dead, having conquered everything but himself!

Alexander had always believed he was descended from Achilles. If that's true, then his Achilles' heel was Alexander's ego.

What good is it for a man to gain the whole world, yet forfeit his soul? Or what can a man give in exchange for his soul? (Mark 8:36–37).

Laughter

Comedian Jerry Lewis calls humor a "safety valve." "The peoples of the world who have the ability to laugh at themselves are those who survive," so says Lewis.

Bob Hope says that laughter has constructive power. "A laugh," he says, "can transform almost unbearable tears into something bearable, even hopeful."

Country humorist Jerry Clower says: "God doesn't want his children to walk around unhappy. He wants them to be happy. I am convinced that there is just one place where there is just not any laughter and that is hell. And I've made arrangements to miss hell, so, ha, ha, I ain't goin' to have to ever be nowhere some folks ain't laughin'!"

The Bible, too, has a whole lot to say about laughter and living with joy. Living with laughter makes you a much better father, Dad! I'm for living with joy and laughter!

Happy laughter and happy family voices in the home will do more to keep kids off the streets at night than the strictest of curfews.

A cheerful heart is good medicine, but a crushed spirit dries up the bones (Prov. 17:22).

Changed Testimony

A farmer was criticized in court for having changed his testimony in a suit he filed against a motorist who had hit his horse-drawn wagon. "Why have you changed your story?" the defense lawyer shouted. "You SAID at the accident scene you weren't hurt. Now you say you were. Why did you tell my client you weren't hurt?"

"Well . . . this is what happened," the farmer patiently explained on the witness stand. "Your client's car knocked me and my horse into a ditch. My horse was on his back, legs in the air, I was on my back, my legs in the air. Your client comes over and says, 'This horse is badly hurt,' and pulls out a .357 magnum and shoots him dead. Then he turned to me and asked, 'Now how about you . . . are you hurt, too?'"

There's nothing like a bit of persuasion to get a man to

change his mind. Accidents do happen and the unexpected may be right around the corner. Are you prepared?

If you think a seat belt is uncomfortable . . .
then perhaps you've never tried a stretcher.

For God so loved the world that He gave his one and only Son, that whoever believes in Him shall not perish but have eternal life (John 3:16).

The acid test of a father's leadership is not in the realm of his social skills, his public relations, his managerial abilities at the office, or how well he handles himself before the public. It is in the home.

Charles R. Swindoll (1936–)

Liberation?

A little boy and girl had just been introduced and were trying to decide what game to play. The boy said, "I have an idea . . . let's play baseball."

But the little girl replied, "Oh, no, I wouldn't do that. Baseball is a boy's game. It's not feminine to run around on a dusty vacant lot. No, I don't want to play baseball."

So the boy said, "Let's play football."

She answered, "Oh, no, that's even less feminine. I might fall and get dirty. No."

He said, "Okay, I've got an idea. I'll race you to the corner and back."

She replied, "No, girl's play quiet games, we don't run and get all sweaty."

He scratched his head, trying to think of what she might

want to do and finally he came up with, "Okay, then, let's play house."

She said, "Good! I'll be the daddy!"

One thing most children save for a rainy
day is lots and lots of energy.

*Sons are a heritage from the Lord, children a
reward from Him. Like arrows in the hands of a
warrior are sons born in one's youth. Blessed is
the man whose quiver is full of them*
(Ps. 127:3–5).

Pillars

Famed English architect Sir Christopher Wren designed a large dome for a church which was so unique that he became the object of criticism among his colleagues. During the construction of this dome, they created so much fuss that the authorities demanded Wren add two huge supporting pillars to keep the dome from collapsing. Wren bitterly objected . . . but the opposition prevailed and the pillars were added!

Fifty years had passed, Wren had died, and the controversial dome needed repainting. When the workers began, they discovered that the two added pillars did not even touch the roof! They were two feet short! Wren had such confidence in his work. The authorities during his lifetime, saw the pillars, assumed they reached the roof, and the controversy died.

They felt secure. Dad . . . just how are you building your life? With false pillars or the real thing?

Faith in order, which is the basis of science, cannot reasonably be separated from faith in an ordainer, which is the basis of religion. (Asa Gray)

By the grace God has given me, I laid a foundation as an expert builder, and someone else is building on it. But each one should be careful how he builds. For no one can lay any foundation other than the one already laid, which is Jesus Christ (1 Cor. 3:10–11).

Build Me a Son

Former General Douglas MacArthur wrote this wonderful prayer:

BUILD ME A SON, O Lord, who will be strong enough to know when he is weak, and brave enough to face himself when he is afraid; one who will be proud and unbending in honest defeat, and humble and gentle in victory.

BUILD ME A SON whose wishes will not take the place of deeds; a son who will know Thee . . . and that to know himself is the foundation stone of knowledge.

LEAD HIM, I pray, not in the path of ease and comfort, but under the stress and spur of difficulties and challenge. Here let him learn to stand up to the storm; here let him learn compassion for those who fail.

And, there's more to this prayer, just turn the page and I'll finish it for you.

Character does not reach its best maturity
until it is controlled, harnessed, and
disciplined.

*My son, do not despise the Lord's
discipline and do not resent His
rebuke, because the Lord disciplines
those he loves, as a father the son he
delights in* (Prov. 3:11–12).

Build Me a Son, II

BUILD ME A SON whose heart will be clear, whose goal will be high, a son who will master himself before he seeks to master other men, one who will reach into the future, yet never forget the past.

AND after all these things are his, add, I pray, enough of a sense of humor so that he may always be serious, yet never take himself too seriously. Give him humility, so that he may always remember the simplicity of true greatness, the open mind of true wisdom, and the meekness of true strength.

THEN, I, his father, will dare to whisper, "I have not lived in vain."

Dad, how about covenanting with me to pray for and seek to build sons and daughters who will be a credit to the human race as well as to their Heavenly Father?!

The true measure of a man is the height of his ideals, the breadth of his sympathy, the depth of his convictions, and the length of his patience.

My son, if you accept my words and store up my commands within you, turning your ear to wisdom and applying your heart to understanding, and if you call out for insight and cry aloud for understanding, and if you look for it as for silver and search for it as for hidden treasure, then you will understand the fear of the Lord and find the knowledge of God (Prov. 2:1–5).

*The father's most important responsibility is
to communicate the real meaning of
Christianity to his children.*

James C. Dobson (1936–)

The Weak Link

In ancient China the people, who had been harassed, invaded, and attacked by the many barbaric hordes to the north of their land, demanded some protection. In desiring this security one of their leaders decided that the best protection for their nation would be to erect what we call the "Great Wall of China." It was built so high they knew no one could climb over it and built so thick that nothing could break it down — quite an engineering feat.

After the wall was built they settled back to enjoy their security. However, during the first 100 years of the wall's existence, China was invaded three times, through the Great Wall! Not once did the barbaric hordes break it down or climb over the top. Each time they bribed a gate-keeper and then marched right through a gate! The Chinese were so busy relying on their walls of stone that they forgot to teach integrity to the children who grew up to guard the gates!

> Rearing kids is like holding a wet bar of soap . . . too firm a grasp and it shoots from your hand, too loose a grasp and it slides away. A gentle but firm grasp keeps it in your control. (Elaine Hannagan)

Train a child in the way he should go, and when he is old he will not turn from it (Prov. 22:6)

The Size of the Fight

A dad was a sales rep and while traveling down the streets of a large city, stopped at a stoplight, happened to look off to his right and saw two boys fighting in a front yard. One boy was quite a bit bigger and obviously getting the upper hand. He was knocking the tar out of the smaller boy. He would punch the smaller guy and blood would spurt from the little guy's nose but he would go right back to take another punch.

This dad decided he should intervene. He pulled his car to the curb and came over yelling at the bigger boy to stop beating up on the little one. But it was the little fellow who responded. He said, "Mister, mind your own business! I ain't got my second wind yet, and when I do I am going to clobber this guy!"

So what's the point? You just can't lick a guy who won't stay down. It's the size of the fight inside which makes the difference in the long run.

The trouble with some men and boys is
that during trying times they stop trying.

*For though a righteous men falls
seven times, he rises again, but the
wicked are brought down by calamity*
(Prov. 24:16).

What Is a Real Man?

God wants men to be free! FREE to demonstrate toughness when a situation or relationship demands it. FREE to display grit, strength, commitment, and decisiveness under the Holy Spirit's direction.

God wants men to be free . . . to demonstrate tenderness, sensitivity, and humility. FREE to be vulnerable enough to foster intimacy and to shed tears. Authentic masculinity produces a divine elasticity in men.

FINALLY, they can lead with firmness, then submit with humility. They can challenge with a cutting edge, then encourage with enthusiasm. They can fight aggressively for a just cause, then moments later weep over suffering. Secure, free, authentic men leave a mark . . . on their colleagues, friends, wives, and ESPECIALLY THEIR CHILDREN.[1]

Every job, including fatherhood, is a self-
portrait of the man who did it . . .
therefore, autograph your life work with
excellence.

*Have I not commanded you? Be
strong and courageous. Do not be
terrified; do not be discouraged, for
the Lord your God will be with you
wherever you go* (Josh. 1:8).

When I was a boy of 14 my father was
so ignorant I could hardly stand to
have the old man around.
But when I got to be 21,
I was astonished at how much
the old man had learned in seven years.

Mark Twain (1835–1910)

The Very Best Gift

A man who was awaiting surgery was visited by his grown son in the hospital. The son said, "Dad, I sure hope you are home for Father's Day this year. I felt awful years ago when I was ten because I never gave you a gift that year."

The father replied, "Son, I remember well the Saturday before that Father's Day. I watched you in the store. I watched as you picked up those fishing lures and stuck them in your pocket. I knew you didn't have any money and I was sad because I thought you were going to walk out of the store without paying. But almost as quickly as you hid them, you pulled them out and put them back on the shelf.

"Then when you stayed outside playing all the next day because you didn't have a present, you probably thought I was hurt. You're wrong, Son . . . when you put those fishing lures back you gave me the best present I've ever received."

You will become as small as your controlling desire; as great as your dominant aspiration. (James Allen)

Now we pray to God that you will not do anything wrong. Not that people will see that we have stood the test but that you will do what is right even though we may seem to have failed (2 Cor. 13:7).

Modern Gift Giving

Two fathers were talking at the office the week preceding Father's Day. The first said, "Hey, this Sunday is Father's Day and my family makes a big fuss over me on this day. My wife makes my favorite breakfast and then my kids each give me a nice gift. I'm really surprised at what beautiful gifts my teenage kids give me every year. Then we all go to church and they take me out to my favorite restaurant for lunch."

"That's real nice," replied the second man. "My wife usually makes a big fuss over me, too. But my kids seem to be a bit different than yours. My oldest teenage son doesn't have a whole lot of ambition. As a matter of fact, this week he said that there was no way he was buying me a Father's Day gift until I paid off the gifts that he charged to my credit card for Mother's Day."

It seems today that when you tell a teenager he must begin shifting for himself, he thinks you're going to buy him a new sports car.

The fear of the Lord is the beginning of knowledge, but fools despise wisdom and discipline (Prov. 1:7).

One Little Detail
Makes the Difference

When Harry was a young man in Louisiana he was always getting into trouble. One morning while waiting for the school bus, he shoved the outhouse into the bayou and went off to school as if nothing had happened.

When he returned his father was waiting for him. He said, "Son, did you push the outhouse into the bayou?"

"Yes, Dad," replied Harry, "like George Washington, I cannot tell a lie."

Harry's dad took off his belt and said, "All right, son, bend over. I'm whipping you."

Harry tried to explain that Mr. Washington didn't spank George when he admitted chopping down the cherry tree.

"Yes, son," said Harry's dad, "but George's father wasn't in the tree."

No one could possibly know as much as a teenager thinks he knows . . . or as little as he thinks his father knows.

I know, my God, that you test the
heart and are pleased with integrity
(1 Chron. 29:17).

Authentic men aren't afraid to show affection, release their feelings, hug their children, cry when they're sad, admit it when they're wrong, and ask for help when they need it.

Charles R. Swindoll (1934–)

The Lady Said "Pew"

A cowboy went to church for the first time in his life. He was enthusiastic about the experience, so he told his friend, "I rode up on my horse and tied him to a tree in the corral."

The friend said, "You don't mean 'corral,' you mean 'parking lot.' "

"Don't know, maybe that's it," he said. "Then I went through the main gate."

"You don't mean main gate, you mean the front door of the church."

"Well, anyway, a couple of fellows took me down the long chute."

"You don't mean the long chute, you mean the center aisle."

"I guess so. Then they put me into one of those little box stalls!"

"You don't mean a box stall, you mean a pew!"

"Oh yes! Now I remember!" said the cowboy. "That's what the lady said when I sat down beside her!"

Too many people spend the first six days of the week sowing wild oats . . . then go to church on Sunday and pray for a crop failure.

Let us not give up meeting together, as some are in the habit of doing, but let us encourage one another . . . and all the more as you see the Day approaching (Heb. 10:25).

Wrong Reactions

During the last turbulent months of Andrew Johnson's presidential administration, a bitter feud erupted between him and General Ulysses S. Grant. The final blow came when Johnson's own party rejected his name at its political convention. Grant was picked and won the presidential election by a large popular majority. Johnson was so embittered that he refused to ride to the inauguration in the same carriage with Grant . . . and did not even attend the swearing-in ceremonies! Johnson never fully recovered from this rejection and died a very bitter, angry man.

Circumstances, tensions, frustrations, failures, rejections, and stresses can push us until we react in bitterness, which is a deadly poison to the soul. It seems as though life is made up of 10 percent of the things that happen to us and 90 percent of our reactions!

Dad . . . be very careful because your reactions are showing!

The difference between success and
failure is how you handle the temptation
to become bitter.

*See to it that no one misses the grace
of God and that no bitter root grows
up to cause trouble and defile many*
(Heb. 12:15).

Flight

Some years ago a bishop of the United Brethren Church was visiting a friend who was the president of a small college. The conversation turned to progress and the college president asked the bishop what he thought would be the next great advancement for mankind. The bishop stated that he felt everything worth inventing had already been invented.

The college president disagreed and voiced this hope, "For one thing, I believe that someday men will be able to fly in the air.

"Nonsense," the bishop objected, "if God had intended man to fly in the air He would have given him wings in the first place."

This conversation probably wouldn't have been recorded for posterity except for one important fact: The bishop's name was Wright. And he had two boys named Orville and Wilbur Wright! The bishop was wrong . . . God did intend for all of us to fly!

Man who say it cannot be done should
not interrupt man doing it.
(Ancient Chinese Proverb)

*But those who hope in the Lord will
renew their strength. They will soar
on wings like eagles; they will run
and not grow weary, they will walk
and not be faint (Isa. 40:31).*

Can't you see the Creator of the universe, who understands every secret, every mystery . . . sitting patiently and listening to a four year old talk to Him? That's a beautiful image of a father.

James C. Dobson (1936–)

The Push

This happened on one of those special cruise ships. A sudden storm blew up at sea and a young lady leaning against the ship's rail lost her balance in the storm on the wet deck and fell overboard. Before anybody could react, another figure plunged into the waves beside her and held her up until a lifeboat could be lowered to rescue them. To everyone's astonishment, the hero was the oldest man on board ship . . . an octogenarian (over 80 for the uninformed) grandfather! That evening he was given a party in honor of his bravery. "Speech . . . speech . . . speech!" the other passengers called out.

The old gentleman rose slowly and looked around at the enthusiastic gathering. "There's just one thing I'd like to know," he said testily, "WHO pushed me?"

So what's the lesson? Sometimes we need a shove to get us doing the right thing!

Courage is something you always have
until you need it.

Be strong and let us fight bravely for
our people and the cities of our God.
The Lord will do what is good in His
sight (2 Sam. 10:12).

My Son

World, take my son by the hand . . . he starts school today! It is all going to be strange and new for a while, and I wish you would sort of treat him gently.

To live in the world will require faith and love and courage. So, world, I wish you would sort of take him by his young hand and teach him the things he will have to know.

He will have to learn, I know, that all men are not just . . . that all men are not true. Teach him that for every scoundrel there is a hero; that for every enemy there is a friend.

Teach him the wonder of books. Teach him that it is far more honorable to fail than to cheat.

The man who penned these words was Abraham Lincoln. These are more than beautiful words, they express a prayer, a prayer that is as contemporary as today. I'm for passing on to our sons and daughters good life lessons.

It's what you learn after you know it all
that counts. (John Wooden)

*Listen to advice and accept
instruction, and in the end you will be
wise* (Prov. 19:20).

What You Are

It was a sunny Saturday afternoon in Minneapolis. My friend and happy father, Jim McGuire, was taking his two boys to play miniature golf. Jim asked at the counter, "How much is it to play?"

The young attendant said, "$4.00 for you and $4.00 for any kid who is eight or older. They get in free if they are under eight. How old are they?"

Jim answered, "The football player's five and the baseball player is eight, so I guess I owe you $8.00, right?"

The young man at the ticket counter said, "Hey, Mister, you could have saved yourself some money. You could have told me the older one is seven and I wouldn't have known the difference."

Jim replied, "Yes, that could be true, but the kids would have known the difference."

Who you are speaks so loudly I can't hear
what you're saying. (Ralph Waldo
Emerson)

*I have set you an example that you
should do as I have done for you*
(John 13:15).

The Down Payment

Richard Loeffler relates this: Having purchased new appliances for our house, my wife and I decided to give our old refrigerator to my parents. When I spoke to my mother on the phone a few days later, she announced, "We want to send you a check for the refrigerator."

"No, Mom, it's a gift," I said. "We want you to have it."

"But you could have sold it," she persisted.

"Look, Mom," I replied. "Just consider it as repayment for all those days that you took care of me while I was in diapers."

After a slight pause, she answered, "In that case, the refrigerator doesn't cover it."

This being a parent works both ways . . . it's being in the middle . . . having parents and being a parent. Both can be joyful and exciting. It's time to also express thanks to our own parents.

Gratitude is not only one of the greatest of
virtues . . . but the parent of all the others.

Be joyful always; pray continually;
give thanks in all circumstances, for
this is God's will for you in Christ
Jesus (1 Thess. 5:16–18).

Fathering is a marathon,
not a sprint.

Paul L. Lewis (1944–)

Where's Dad?

Expanding the role of fatherhood is one of the hot topics of today which goes right along with a persistent divorce rate. What effect does one have on the other after kids are grown up?

The answer is uncontested — divorce has produced some very negative effects on a father's contact with adult kids. Also, more than twice as many married as divorced fathers have adult children living with them. Only half of divorced fathers have weekly contact with at least one adult child compared with 90 percent of married fathers.

Even more distressing . . . one-third of divorced fathers have lost all contact with one or more of their adult children! All of the above statistics have come out of a study by Dr. Teresa Cooney as written in *Better Families* (9/93).

Dad, the best thing you can do for your kids is to love their mother.

Sometimes a man imagines that he will lose himself if he gives himself, and keep himself if he hides himself. But the contrary takes place with terrible exactitude. (Ernest Hello)

For this reason a man will leave his father and mother and be united to his wife, and they will become one flesh (Gen. 2:24).

Determination

Uncle Bud Robinson at times was an embarrassment to his denomination, in fact, he might have embarrassed the whole lot of us, too. One time, when asked to pray at a very solemn church gathering, he prayed this prayer:

"Oh, Lord, give me a backbone like a saw log, ribs like the sleepers under this church, put iron shoes on my feet, galvanize my britches, hang a wagon load of determination in the gable end of my soul. Help me to sign a contract to fight the devil as long as I have a vision, bite him as long as I have a tooth and when I have no teeth, let me gum him till I die!"

Determination! Martin Luther must have been cut from the same piece of cloth when he prayed like this: "Here I stand, what I have said, I have said! Let the Pope roar! Let the Vatican scream! Here I stand, so help me God!"

It is cynicism and fear that freeze life; it is faith that thaws it out, releases it, sets it free. (Harry Emerson Fosdick)

Pray also for me, that whenever I open my mouth, words may be given me so that I will fearlessly make known the mystery of the Gospel, for which I am an ambassador in chains. Pray that I may declare it fearlessly, as I should (Eph. 6:19–20).

Cookie

Harry "Cookie" Lavagetto, former major league baseball player and manager died Friday, August 10, 1990. He was 77. *So what? . . .* you may be thinking.

Cookie managed the old Washington Senators from 1957-1960 and was the very first manager of the Minnesota Twins. He was a .269 lifetime hitter. But his great moment in the sun came in 1947 as a member of the Brooklyn Dodgers. In the fourth game of the World Series, New York Yankees pitcher Floyd Bevens was throwing a no-hitter. With two outs in the ninth, Lavagetto had a double hit off the right field wall (which was his very last hit in the majors) to drive in two runs and lead the Dodgers to a 3-2 win.

Years later, he was asked if he was thinking about breaking up that no-hitter when he hit the ball. Replied Lavagetto, "Son, I wasn't thinking no-hitter, I was thinking double!"

Every man is enthusiastic at times. One man has enthusiasm for 30 minutes . . . another man has it for 30 days, but it is the man who has it for 30 years who makes a success of life. (Edward B. Butler)

Brothers, I do not consider myself yet to have taken hold of it. But one thing I do: Forgetting what is behind and straining toward what is ahead, I press on toward the goal to win the prize (Phil. 3:13–14).

One of the best legacies
a father can leave his children
is to love their mother.

C. Neil Strait

Never Die

Since General MacArthur made his famous statement, "Old soldiers never die, they just fade away," many more interesting quotes have been proposed such as these:

Old postmen never die, they just lose their zip.

Old scoutmasters never die, they just smell that way.

Old deans never die, they just lose their faculties.

Old doctors never die, they just lose their patience.

Old preachers never die, they just never conclude.

Old ballplayers never die, they just strike out.

Old gardeners never die, they just compost.

In order to live right, we need a healthy outlook on aging and dying. Therefore in order to live right, we must prepare to die right.

Everyone should fear death until he has
something that will live on after his death.

Just as man is destined to die once,
and after that to face judgment, so
Christ was sacrificed once to take
away the sins of many people
(Heb. 9:27–28).

New Laws

Are you aware that there is now a 'NEW OFFICIAL RULE' book? It's an answer to "Murphy's Law." Let me share some of these with you. . . .

AGNES ALLEN'S LAW: "Almost anything is easier to get into than out of." (Agnes Allen)

BARNES' LAW OF PROBABILITY: "There's a 50 percent chance of anything . . . either it happens or it doesn't." (Michael R. Barnes)

CLONINGER'S LAW: "In a country as large as the United States it is possible to find at least 50 people who will believe, buy, try, or practice anything." (Dale O. Cloninger)

And how about one more? This was read while waiting for my wife to finish shopping in a supermarket and was taken from the label placed on jars of Hellmann's mayonnaise. We call it HELLMAN'S PRINCIPLE: "Keep cool, but do not freeze!"

If Murphy's Law can go wrong, it will, and it will do so exactly when you want to show its accuracy. (Onesimo T. Almeida)

What has been will be again, what has been done will be done again; there is nothing new under the sun (Eccles. 1:9).

Straight Paths

One beautiful, bright, sunny, winter day, when snow had just covered the ground with a fresh new blanket . . . a father went walking with his son. Seeing a large tree some distance away on a little hill, he said to his son, "I'll race you to that tree, but before we start, I want you to know that this is not a race to see who will get to the tree first. It's a race to see who can make the straightest path in the snow."

This appealed to the son because he knew his father's longer legs would beat him. He made up his mind to walk it straight. He looked at his feet and carefully placed one in front of the other. When he got to the tree, Dad was already there. But he saw something he hadn't expected when they looked back. His father had walked the straightest path because Dad knew that if he kept his eyes on the goal without looking down, he'd walk a straight line!

Training children to walk the straight and narrow path is easy for fathers . . . all they have to do is lead the way.

But small is the gate and narrow the road that leads to life, and only a few find it (Matt. 7:14).

You don't need to be right all the time.
Your child wants a man for a father,
not a formula. He wants real parents,
real people, capable of making mistakes
without moping about it.

C.D. Williams

Fatherly Advice

The ancient philosopher Socrates wrote: "Could I climb to the highest place in Athens, I would lift up my voice and proclaim: FELLOW CITIZENS, why do you turn and scrape every stone to gather wealth, and take so little care of the children, to whom you must someday relinquish it all?"

The contemporary times of Socrates and ancient Athens, according to historians, were much like ours in that they were affluent, morally corrupt and spiritually decadent. Socrates is thought to have been born in 470 B.C. and died in 399 B.C. at the age of 71. Here, he is talking of his great concern for the children of Athens. What did he mean? Likely, that parents were spoiling the younger generation with too many material goods while neglecting their spiritual and moral training. Sounds too much like our day. Dad, it's time to also put some moral and spiritual values into little heads while they are young.

No man sends a more confusing message
than the father who gives good advice
while setting a bad example.

*My son, preserve sound judgment and
discernment, do not let them out of
your sight; they will be life for you*
(Prov. 3:21–22).

Violent Homes

One of the deadliest places in America is the average home. Acts of domestic violence occur every nine seconds in the U.S. About half of all couples will experience at least one violent incident. In 1/4 of these couples, violence is a common occurance. Twenty percent of all murders are committed within the family, 13 percent by spouses. Most family violence is committed against women. Men commit 95 percent of all spousal assaults. Twenty-one percent of all women who use the hospital emergency room are there because they are battered. Six million American women are beaten each year by their husbands or boyfriends — 4,000 of them are killed! Battering or physical abuse is the single major cause of injury to women, more frequent than auto accidents, muggings, and rapes combined. One in four female suicides was a victim of family violence.

Victims of domestic violence are three times more likely to be victimized again than victims of other types of crimes!

Sir, it's time that all of us men help put a stop to this abuse!

A society that does not bow down to worship Almighty God begins to literally come apart because it cannot deal with the tremendous burden of sin. Individually and corporately, we start to come apart. (Peter Marshall)

Husbands, love your wives, just as Christ loved the church and gave himself up for her . . . in this same way, husbands ought to love their wives as their own bodies (Eph. 5:25).

The Greatest Preacher

There is a wonderful story found in the biography of G. Campbell Morgan. He had four sons, all of whom followed in their father's footsteps to become preachers. The youngest, Howard, considered to be a great preacher in his own right, once spoke in his father's place on this side of the Atlantic while Dr. Morgan ministered in London.

Someone came to the house when the family was there, and thinking to find out what Howard was "made of," asked the question: "Howard, who is the greatest preacher in your family?"

Howard, who had a great admiration for his father, looked across the room at him and without a moment's hesitation answered, "My mother!"

Howard was right . . . it's often the person who never graces a platform or pulpit who may be the greatest at living out the truth, practicing the truth, or speaking out the truth.

Example is not the main thing in
influencing others, especially children.
It's the only thing.

*Who is it he is trying to teach? To
whom is he explaining his message?
To children. . . . For it is: Do and do,
do and do, rule on rule, rule on rule;
a little here, a little there*
(Isa. 28:9–10).

*The best way for a child to learn to fear
God is to know a real Christian.
The best way for a child to learn to pray
is to live with a father and mother
who know a life of friendship with God
and who truly pray.*

Johann Heinrich Pestalozzi (1746–1827)

Where Credit Is Due

To the man who is actually in the arena, who strives valiantly . . . who knows the great enthusiasms, the great devotions . . . and spends himself in a worthy cause . . . who at the best, knows the triumph of high achievement; and who, at the worst, if he fails . . . at least fails while daring greatly, so that his place shall never be with those cold and timid souls . . . who know neither victory nor defeat.

Stirring words . . . they are a paragraph left to us by former President Teddy Roosevelt, who was a man who practiced what he preached.

The biblical writer James would have approved of such a lifestyle. He was the Bible writer who challenged us to put our living into practice. He was the man who said that words without actions to back them up amount to nothing. It's real living in the arena of life where the rubber hits the road.

Do something! Quit talking about it!
Either lead, follow, or get out of the way!

*You see that his faith and his actions
were working together, and his faith
was made complete by what he did*
(James 2:22).

The Opening Ceremony

Grand openings are to be impressive events. Consider when Brigham City, Utah, finished a new pistol range for their police training program, they wished to open it with style. Officials invited a crack team of marksmen from the Utah Peace Force to do the honors, the idea being that one of them would, with a flourish, fire one shot breaking the ceremonial ribbon.

It was something to behold! Some 500 shots later, the ceremonial ribbon remained intact! An eyewitness reported that it was finally cut when an officer stepped up at close range and blasted it with a shotgun, leaving the ribbon smoking in shambles!

Something about the best devices of men and mice comes to mind. I'm for learning to laugh at ourselves when life and plans don't always go as planned. And as long as all of us are human we will mess things up. How to handle that? Humor and an honest act of forgiveness goes a long way.

To err is human, but to really mess things up in today's world takes a computer.

For if you forgive men when they sin against you, your heavenly Father will also forgive you. But if you do not forgive men their sins, your Father will not forgive your sins (Matt. 6:14–15).

The Architectural Award

Kansas City proudly had completed the new Kemper Arena in 1979. The American Institute of Architects had previously awarded their prestigious prize to it as "one of the finest buildings in the nation." In planning for their annual conference, they decided to take it to Kansas City so they could be near this structure. The first day of their conference hundreds of architects toured this inspired structure. The publication, *ARCHITECTURAL RECORD*, described the building as having "an almost awesome muscularity."

On the second day of the conference, the Kemper Arena collapsed in a dramatic heap of roof and beams! No one was hurt . . . which was about the only positive thing to come out of this colossal event!

This, among a whole lot of other things, is to help us understand that human beings are not infallible!

A fool tells you what he will do . . . a boaster, what he has done. The wise man does it and says nothing.

Do not boast about tomorrow, for you do not know what a day may bring forth. Let another praise you, and not your own mouth; someone else, and not your own lips
(Prov. 27:1–2).

Build me a son, O Lord,
who will be strong enough to know
when he is weak and brave enough
to face himself when he is afraid,
one who will be proud and unbending
in honest defeat, and humble and gentle
in victory.

Douglas MacArthur (1880–1964)

Ultimate Seduction

Leo Tolstoy tells a story about a Russian who fell heir to his father's small farm. One morning as he stood near the homestead, a stranger, a person of authority, told him he could have, for nothing, all the land he could walk around in one day. BUT — by sundown he had to have returned to the starting point. The young man, eager, threw off his coat and started across the rich fields. His first plan was to cover a tract 6 miles square . . . but when he'd walked 6, he decided to make it 9, then 12, then 15 . . . a total of 60 miles before sundown.

By noon he'd covered 30 miles . . . he didn't bother to stop for water or food, but hurried on as fast as he could force himself to walk. Fatigue began to set in. The sun was beginning to set. He hurried more. A few hundred yards from the finish he started to feel faint but managed to force himself to stagger across the line where the stranger stood, and fell dead.

The stranger said, "I offered him all the land he could cover. Now you see what that is: six feet long and two feet wide."

Any man who thinks money is everything has never been sick or faced death.

Then He said to them, "Watch out! Be on your guard against all kinds of greed; a man's life does not consist in the abundance of his possessions" (Luke 12:15).

Mother Says "No"

During the American Revolutionary War, an officer was sent around the Virginia countryside to confiscate horses for military use. He came to a fine old mansion, rang the bell, and asked to speak to the mistress.

"Madame," he said to the dignified elderly lady he met in the parlor, "I am claiming your horses on orders from my commander."

"Sir," she answered, "You cannot have my horses. I need them for the spring plowing. Who is your commander?"

"General George Washington, commander of the American army."

"You just go back and tell General George Washington that his mother says he cannot have her horses," she replied with a smile.

One of the magic words that parents need to use today is "NO"!

I know you believe you understand what
you think I said, but I'm not sure you
realize that what you heard is not what I
meant.

*Simply let your "Yes" be "Yes," and
your "No" "No;" anything beyond
this comes from the evil one*
(Matt. 5:37).

A Child's Theology

A new children's encyclopedia salesman was working his way door-to-door and was in a home concluding his presentation to the father of a five-year-old boy. The salesman sensed he had already convinced this father of the value of this set of books for his son. But he went on to use one of his high-powered, highly charged closing techniques.

"If the answer to any question your little boy asks can't be found in this encyclopedia, I will refuse to sell this set to you," he said to the father. Then, turning to the five-year-old, he dramatically asked, "Ask me a question, sonny, any question. Just ask me anything you want to know and I'll show your dad where he can find the answer in this wonderful encyclopedia set."

The five year old thought, then asked, "What kind of car does God drive?"

The salesman received an educational experience . . . he never asked that question again of a five year old!

Having children is like having a bowling alley installed in your brain. (Martin Mull)

You know the commandments: "Do not commit adultery, do not murder, do not steal, do not give false testimony, honor your father and mother" (Luke 18:20).

Endnotes

[1]*Moody Monthly, June 1990.*